HAL•LEONARD

pro vocal®
BETTER THAN KARAOKE!

VOLUME 13

Frank Sinatra
CLASSICS

Cover photo courtesy of Photo...

ISBN-13: 978-1-4234-0502-3
SBN-10: 1-4234-0502-1

HAL•LEONARD®
CORPORATION
7777 W. BLUEMOUND RD. P.O. BOX 13819 MILWAUKEE, WI 53213

Visit Hal Leonard Online at
www.halleonard.com

Frank Sinatra CLASSICS

CONTENTS

All the Way

Words by Sammy Cahn
Music by James Van Heusen

if you __ let me love you, __ it's for sure I'm gon-na love you

all _____ the way,

Interlude

all _____ the way.

3. So,

Outro

if you __ let me love you, __ it's for sure I'm __ gon-na love you

all the way, ___ all the

way. _____

6

I've Got the World on a String

Lyric by Ted Koehler
Music by Harold Arlen

Intro
Freely

N.C. Bb13#11   A13   Bb7   A13

1. I've _____ got the

Verse

D   C7   B   Em   A7   F#m7

world _____ on a string.   Sit-tin' on a rain-bow,   got the string a-

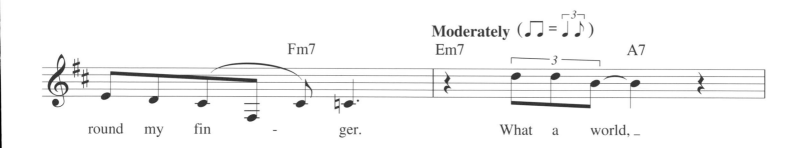

Fm7   **Moderately** (♫ = ♩♪)   Em7   A7

round my fin - ger.   What a world, _____

Em7   A13   D6   B7b9#5

what a life, _____   I'm in love. _____

Verse

Em9   A7#9#5   D   C7   B7

2. I've got a song that I sing, _____   I

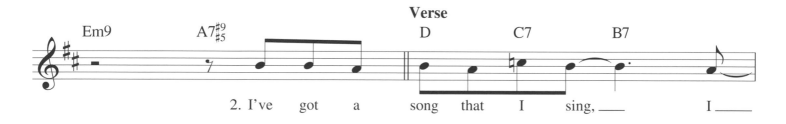

Em7   A7   F#m   F#m7   Fm7

_____ can make the rain go   an - y - time _____ I move _____ my fin - ger,

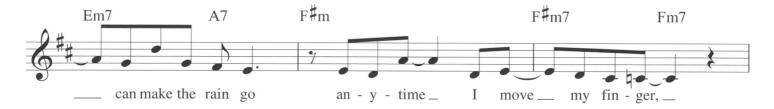

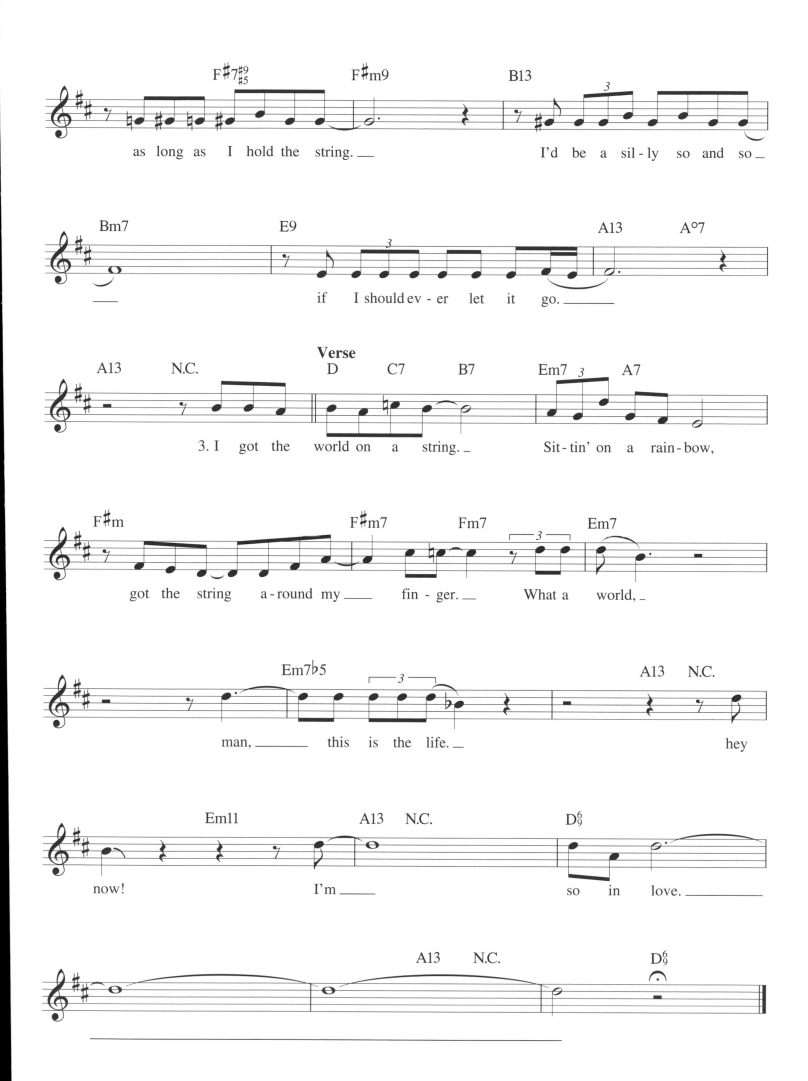

The Birth of the Blues

Words by B.G. DeSylva and Lew Brown
Music by Ray Henderson

I've Got You Under My Skin

Words and Music by Cole Porter

The Lady Is a Tramp

Words by Lorenz Hart
Music by Richard Rodgers

Bridge

free, _____ fresh _____ wind __ in her

hair, life _____ with - out care.

She's broke, and it's oke.

Outro-Verse

Hates Cal - i - for - nia, _____ it's so cold and so

damp. That's why the la - dy, _____

that's why the la - dy, _____ that's why the la -

- dy, she's __ a tramp. _____

Time After Time

from the Metro-Goldwyn-Mayer Picture IT HAPPENED IN BROOKLYN
Words by Sammy Cahn
Music by Jule Styne

Verse

2. I on-ly know _____ what I know, the pass-ing years will show _____ you've kept my love so young, so new, _____ and time _____ af-ter time, _____ you'll hear me say that I'm _____ so luck-y to be lov-ing _____ you.

Interlude

Outro-Verse

I on-ly know _____ what I know, _____ the

pass - ing years _____ will show _____ you've

kept my love so young, so new, _____

_____ and time _____ af - ter time _____ you'll

hear me say that I'm so luck - y to be

lov - ing _____ you. _____

Theme From
"New York, New York"

Words by Fred Ebb
Music by John Kander

an - y - where. ___ It's up to you New _____

York, New York. _____

New _____ York, _

___ New _____ York. _____ I want to

Bridge

wake up in a cit - y that nev - er sleeps,

and find I'm "A" ____ num - ber one, top of the list,

Slowly

king of the hill, ___ "A" num - ber one. _____ 4. These lit - tle town _

Witchcraft

Lyric by Carolyn Leigh
Music by Cy Coleman